Prima Princessa

BALLET *for* BEGINNERS

FEATURING THE
SCHOOL OF
AMERICAN BALLET

imagine!
Publishing

Library of Congress Control Number: 2011924429

10 9 8 7 6 5 4 3 2 1

An Imagine Book
Published by Charlesbridge
85 Main Street
Watertown, MA 02472
617-926-0329
www.charlesbridge.com

School of American Ballet photographs by Dan Howell
Creative movement class photography by David Baumbach
This book is written and illustrated by Prima Princessa Productions, LLC

Printed and manufactured in China, May 2011
All rights reserved

ISBN: 978-1-936140-45-9

Table of Contents

Yoo-hoo!

It's me, Prima Princessa. Come join me as we explore the wonderful world of ballet!

ballet is a beautiful form of dance that dates back hundreds of years. Did you know that ballet actually started out during the Italian Renaissance in the 1400s as a dance form imitating men fighting with swords? Classical ballet technique wasn't developed until the 1600s. King Louis XIV of France created the first official school of ballet in 1661, and the names of the steps created by his school are still used today in ballet classes worldwide.

There are no words in ballet, so dancers have to use their bodies to tell the story. Ballerinas always look so magical as they twirl and leap across the stage. How do they do it? Ballet dancers train long and hard to learn the many steps that make up the classical art form of ballet.

In this book we'll see many of these steps demonstrated by my wonderful friends. We'll start with a trip to a Pre-Ballet or **Creative**

Afterward, we'll head over to the Children's Ballet Division and the Advanced Ballet classes at the **School of American Ballet** at Lincoln Center in New York City, NY. The School of American Ballet, or SAB, is the official academy of the New York City Ballet. It was founded in 1934 by the famous choreographer George Balanchine and supporter of the arts Lincoln Kirstein. SAB is a world renowned ballet school. Its dancers often go on to dance for the New York City Ballet as well as other top companies worldwide.

Movement class for young dancers. It's hard not to want to take a ballet class once you've seen a ballet live on stage. Ballerinas are so graceful, and their costumes are so beautiful! But most dancers under six aren't ready to learn difficult ballet positions. What they can do is join a Creative Movement class like the one we'll soon see. Creative Movement is all about making new friends, having fun dancing, and getting a taste of what a real ballet class will be like.

Ballet is a fantastic activity that will teach you how, with hard work and patience, you can achieve your goals. It will give you confidence, strength, poise, and grace. Most importantly, ballet is lots of fun! Now let's go learn about it!

Creative Movement

Look how much fun the girls are having!

Welcome to Mr. Chris's Creative Movement class! Most dance classes take place inside a dance studio with a wooden floor, a barre, and mirrors, but Mr. Chris has decided to take advantage of the beautiful weather and hold class outside. The girls are so excited to be out in the fresh air. The grass feels great between their toes!

Mr. Chris starts the class by asking everyone to sit down on the ground around him. This is **circle time**. When you take a Creative Movement class, it will probably start with circle time, too. Then you'll do some stretching before getting to the best part of all: dancing! Mr. Chris is welcoming all the girls. He's going around the circle and asking each girl to say her name. This helps everyone get to know one another. It won't be long before they're all dancing and having fun together.

Creative Movement class is a great place to make friends.

musicality

Music can make you feel happy or sad. It can make you feel excited or calm. One of the main goals of a Creative Movement class is to teach students a sense of **musicality**. Musicality in dance means being able to move your body expressively to music. You have to listen carefully to hear how the mood of a piece of music changes. Then you have to change the way your body is moving to match the new mood of the music. In Creative Movement class, your teacher will have you moving in all sorts of ways to all sorts of music. You'll be running, jumping, skipping, and spinning to happy music, sad music, fast music, slow music, and more!

Faster! Faster!

Mr. Chris's class is getting into the spirit of some fast-paced, lively music by skipping around together in a circle. That looks like fun! The music is going fast now, but Mr. Chris will slow it down soon so the girls can practice dancing at different speeds. The girls move their bodies to match the **tempo**, or speed of the music.

Dancing with friends is a great way to get in touch with the spirit of the music. As you dance, your body will relax and you will start to move naturally to the music, developing your musicality.

Watch your head!

Mr. Chris has taught the girls how to make a bridge. Two girls hold up their arms as the rest of the girls slowly tiptoe underneath to the music. The girls love dancing together. They'll be taking turns holding their arms up and going under the bridge.

It's fun to pretend to be a ballerina! Mr. Chris has taught Kimberly some basic arm movements. These movements are very similar to some of the arm positions she'll learn when she gets a bit older and moves into ballet class. Right now, Mr. Chris just wants Kimberly to get a sense of how she can use her arms to express herself. There will be lots of time to worry about technique, or exact positioning of her body, later. Why don't you try these positions? Remember, musicality is all about moving your body expressively to the music.

Kimberly's arms look so graceful! She'll be a ballerina in no time!

I make a great butterfly!

Explaining Pantomime

Ririko and Dede
love to dress up.

Ballets have no words, but they usually tell
a story. Dancers use their bodies to show
how they are feeling, and pretend to be
different things to show what is happening
in the story. Pretending like this is called
pantomime.

Ririko makes a wonderful butterfly, too.

In Creative Movement class, you will pretend to be all sorts of different things. Your teacher may ask you to pretend to be rain, a car, a bunny, a princess, or even a flower blooming!

The girls in Mr. Chris's class are pretending to be butterflies. They've even changed into their butterfly costumes, complete with wings! Costumes aren't just for fun. It's easier to pretend to be something when you're dressed up like it. In ballet, dancers get to wear all sorts of costumes. In fact, the ballerinas usually change their costumes a few times per show!

Mr. Chris is showing the girls how to move their arms slowly up and down like beautiful butterflies fluttering around a garden.

"Look at us, Prima Princessa! We're flying, just like you!"

expressiveness in dance

facial expressions are a very important part of pantomime. The face can be used to show all sorts of emotions, and dancers spend lots of time practicing different expressions. The audience is usually sitting far away, so dancers really need to exaggerate their expressions so that they can be seen.

In Creative Movement class your teacher will have you practice showing lots of different emotions. Sometimes you'll even get to practice in front of a mirror. Think about how different people look when they are happy or sad. How do they hold their heads? What shapes are their mouths? Are their eyes looking at you or are they looking down?

What great faces, girls! Faye, Allison, Cristina, and Sarah are showing us their best happy, sad, surprised, and mad faces. Can you make these faces, too?

Cristina has stretched her mouth wide open to show how surprised she is. Her eyes are big and round.

Faye looks so happy. Her eyes are sparkling and her mouth is shaped in a big smile.

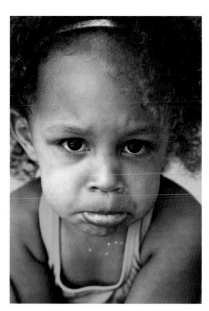

Look at how Allison's lip is curled up. She's got this sad expression down!

Watch out! Sarah's got on her mad face! See how she's squinting her eyes and scrunching her forehead?

Children's Ballet Class

for students 6 to 13 years old

The girls are dressed in their leotards and tights, all ready to go.

dress Code for ballet class

It's time to visit the School of American Ballet (SAB) in New York City. We'll be starting with a visit to their Children's Ballet Division. Many ballet companies have their own ballet schools, but you can study at a regular studio, too. No matter where you attend class, it's important to ask your teacher ahead of time what you should wear. Girls usually wear pink tights and a leotard. Boys wear white T-shirts with either black bike shorts or black tights.

You'll also need proper ballet shoes, called ballet slippers. Ballet slippers are pink for girls and white or black for boys. Girls are also required to pull their hair back in a tight bun. This keeps their hair up and out of their faces and allows their necks to be seen. You shouldn't wear jewelry to class, either, because it could get in the way of your dancing.

Your outfit may feel a bit strange at first, but soon you'll be able to quickly pull your hair back in a tight bun, and you'll get used to your leotard and ballet slippers.

The girls are fixing their hair before class.

Posture and Stretching

Starting at the age of six, ballet class takes place in a real dance studio. In your first few years of class, you'll develop good posture and learn all of the basic positions and steps of ballet. You'll probably attend class twice a week for an hour each class. Beginner ballet class is much more structured than Creative Movement class.

The first and most important thing in dance is posture. Take a look at my posture. See how I'm holding myself straight, tall, and balanced? Ballet dancers have to have perfect posture in order to keep their balance in all of the difficult turns and other dance steps they perform.

Kaitlyn's teacher Katrina Killian adjusts her posture, just a smidge.

Wow, the splits!

A ballerina's strength and balance come from the center of her body. Imagine you are a wooden horse on a merry-go-round with a pole going straight through the middle of your body. The pole starts at the center of your lower back and goes up through your head, holding you up high and keeping your hips, shoulders, and head all in a straight line. This is the perfect ballet posture.

Once you're standing up straight, breathe and relax. It is important to breathe smoothly and deeply, and not to tense up your body, or you will look stiff and not very graceful.

turnout and pointing your feet

turnout

The first thing you'll learn in ballet is how to turn your hips and feet outward. This is called **turnout**. With perfect turnout, your feet will point in opposite directions from each other to form a straight line, with the heels touching. Dancers work on keeping and improving their turnout throughout their training. You should never force your turnout, or you could really hurt your legs and hips.

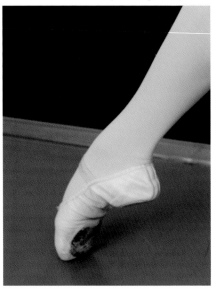

Here's how you point your foot.

pointing your feet

All ballet dancers learn how to point their feet to make long, graceful lines with their legs. You have to point your feet for almost every movement you do. Just like with turnout, a beautiful point will become easier after many years of practice. Try pointing your feet whenever you can: while you are sitting at home watching TV, underneath the dinner table while you are eating, or even laying in bed.

Bianca is pointing her foot and Margot is showing us her great turnout.

Good job girls!
Your turnout looks
wonderful.

Class has started and the students have begun their exercises at the **barre**. A barre is a long, rounded piece of wood that extends along the length of the studio. It's usually set up next to a mirror so that you can check your positioning while you stretch. Barre exercises warm up your muscles and stretch them out so you don't hurt yourself when doing more complicated steps later in class. Hold on to the barre for support so that you can concentrate on moving and holding different parts of your body still. Barre exercises are always done first in one direction and then in the other so that both sides of your body are stretched equally.

the basic positions

There are five basic foot positions in ballet. There are also five basic arm positions. These **positions** form the basis for all of ballet. It takes time to master the positions, and ballet dancers practice them daily. Each of the arm positions can be used with the feet in any of the five positions. For example, during a warm-up at the barre, your feet might be in first position while your arms are posed in fifth position.

first position (en première)

In first position, the balls of the feet are turned out completely. The heels touch each other and the feet face outward, forming a straight line.

To hold your arms in first position, curve them in front of your body. Hold your arms up in front of you as if you are forming a circle.

First position feet

Second position arms and feet

second position (en seconde)

In second position for the feet, the balls of both feet are turned out completely, with the heels separated by the length of one foot. This is similar to first position, but the feet are spread apart.

For second position arms, open your arms to your sides. Keep your arms slightly rounded, like in first position. Make a gentle slope from your shoulder to the tips of your fingers by lowering your elbows slightly below shoulder level and keeping your wrists at the same level as your elbows. Keep your shoulders down, your neck long, and your chin up.

third position (en troisième)

The School of American Ballet no longer teaches third position as one of the primary positions because it is not used in most ballet choreography, but lots of other schools still teach third as a position. In fact, I'm doing it right now. In third position, one foot is placed in front of the other foot. The heel of the front foot should touch the middle of the back foot.

See how I'm holding my arms? This is third position for arms. Curve one arm over your head, as in fifth position, and one arm to the side, as in second position.

fourth position (en quatrième)

In fourth position, the toes of each foot are lined up with the heel of the other foot, but the legs are separated by approximately the length of one foot.

The arms work opposite the legs. Bring your right arm forward, rounded, at the same height as your chest. Raise your left arm above your head in a slightly rounded position.

Fourth position
arms and feet

Fifth position arms and feet

fifth position (en cinquième)

In fifth position, both feet touch, with the toes of each foot reaching the heel of the other.

For fifth position arms, lift your arms over your head, but not too far back. You should be able to see the palms of your hands without moving your head. Round your arms by slightly bending your elbows. Your hands should be close together but your fingers shouldn't touch. Make sure the palms of your hands are facing inward. As you reach the more advanced levels of ballet, you will see that there are actually two positions of the arms in fifth position: low and high fifth.

plié and relevé

Demi-plié and grand plié

the students are practicing their **pliés** and **relevés**.

Pliés stretch your leg muscles during warm-up and help to improve your turnout. They are very important because they teach you how to bend your knees when you are connecting different steps. There are two types of pliés: **demi-pliés** and **grand pliés**. Both are done during warm-up in all of the basic positions, from first to fifth.

demi-plié (duh-MEE-plee-AY)

The demi-plié is a half bend at the knees and should be done in two counts going down and two counts coming up. The demi-plié is used in almost every ballet step. It is important to hold your back straight and your shoulders straight and front. Pliés should be practiced in each of the five positions.

grand plié (grahn plee-AY)

The grand plié is a full bend at the knees and should be done in four counts going down and four counts coming up. Release your heels when you reach a full bend (except in the second position, when they remain on the floor) and then push them back down to the floor as you pass through a demi-plié and come to the standing position.

Relevé

relevé (rel-ah-VAY)

Relevés help you develop strength in your legs and feet. This is important because you'll need strong legs and feet for more advanced work and when you learn jumps. Relevés can be done in any of the five positions. For relevé in first, start in first position and smoothly lift both of your heels as far off the floor as you can at the same time. When you've reached the balls of your feet, called "demi-pointe," slowly go back down and end again in first position.

battement
tendu

Start and end in fifth posiion

battement tendu (baht-MAHN tahn-DEW):
front, side, and back

Battement tendu is a wonderful exercise for strengthening the legs and feet. This barre exercise is generally repeated several times with each leg. "**Battement**" is French for "beating," while "**Tendu**" means "stretch." Battement tendu can be done from several different starting positions. Slide your foot in a straight line out to either the front for battement tendu front, to the side for battement tendu side, or to the back for battement tendu back. Hold your knees tight once the leg is fully extended and pointed, then slide your foot back to the starting position.

Tendu back

Tendu front

Tendu side

Passé

passé and sur le cou-de-pied

passé (pah-SAY)

Passé refers to both a position and a movement. As a position, one foot is placed in front or in back of the other knee, with the toes touching the knee. As a movement, the **working foot**—the foot that is moving—passes the front or back of the knee of the standing leg. Slide your foot up the front of your leg until your toes reach your knee and then pass your foot to the back of your knee and slide it back down to fifth position.

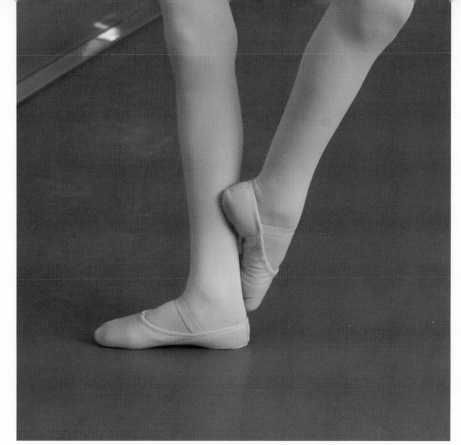

Sur le cou-de-pied

sur le cou-de-pied
(sir luh coo-duh-PYAY)

In this position, wrap your working foot around the ankle of your other leg. Sur le cou-de-pied is a French term that means "on the neck of the foot."

rond de jambe

rond de jambe à terre (ron duh jahm ah tare)

Rond de jambe à terre teaches you how to move your leg in a circular pattern.

Starting in first position, with your hand on the barre, stand up straight on your supporting leg and slide your other foot out into tendu front. Move your leg to tendu side and then to tendu back, creating a sweeping circular pattern.

rond de jambe en dedans (ron duh jahm on duh-dahn)

In **rond de jambe en dedans**, the foot does the reverse movements, starting with tendu back and moving toward the front.

1.

Rond de jambe à terre

développé

this unfolding movement can be done at the barre or without the barre. For **développé** (day-vel-o-PAY), start in fifth position. Place one foot into sur le cou-de-pied. Then slide the foot up the front of the leg to the knee. Extend your leg as you raise your arms. Hold your leg still for a moment and then lower it.

Center Work

In order to develop good balance and technique, ballet dancers spend half of each class performing exercises in the center of the room, without any support from the barre. This set of exercises is similar to those done at the barre and is called **center work**. My friends from SAB have begun their center work.

Écarté (ay-car-TAY) means "wide apart" or "open." Your body is open, making a flat line. Face one front corner of the room and point your leg to the other front corner. Hold your arms in fourth position, with your head looking behind your raised arm.

Effacé (ay-fa-SAY) means "turned away." In effacé, your legs will look open to the audience. For effacé front, face front and turn your body toward the front left corner of the studio. Tendu front with your left foot. Hold your arms in fourth position with your right arm over your head and tilt your neck to the right.

Écarté   Effacé

En face (on foss) means "facing the front." Your arms and legs can be in any position while your body completely faces the front of the room.

Your arms look so graceful!

Croisé (qua-say) means "crossed," because your legs will look crossed to the audience. Face front and turn your body toward the front left corner of the studio. Tendu front with your right foot. Hold your arms in fourth position with your left arm over your head and tilt your neck to the right.

En face   Croisé

b + pose

the **B+** is very elegant. Stand on either foot with your other leg behind you. Your rear leg should be slightly bent and placed behind your standing foot with your knees touching. The big toe on your back leg should be touching the floor. B+ is used regularly in ballet as a standing position for the **corps de ballet**.

"Corps de ballet" is French for "body of the ballet." Ballet companies are made up of principal dancers and soloists who dance the leading roles and the corps de ballet. The corps dancers perform the group dances and can work together to make many patterns and shapes on the stage.

B+ actually got its name from an SAB dancer named Barbara. Barbara had just rehearsed a ballet and was writing her steps in a notebook so that she would remember them. Back then, this pose didn't have a name. Barbara needed to write something in her notebook and decided to call it "B+." The "B" was for "Barbara," and the "+" looked a little bit like the shape the legs make when the dancer stands in this position. B+ was named!

pas de Chat

This adorable jumping step is a petite allegro, or little jump, quite like a cat leaping. In French, "**pas de chat**" (pah duh shah) means "step of the cat."

Starting in fifth position and looking in the direction you are moving, lift your back foot to your calf and plié on your front leg. Then jump into the air, picking up both legs at once underneath your body, and point your feet toward each other. Land on one bent leg with your other leg pointing to the mid-shin. Finish in fifth position.

3.

4.

Advanced Ballet Class
for students 14 and older

If you dream of having a career as a professional ballerina, intensive training begins at eight years old. There are two ways to study ballet once you have progressed to an advanced training level: you could go to your local middle school for academics and then study ballet with a highly qualified local ballet instructor after school, or you could audition for a full-time ballet school.

My advanced ballet friends are all full-time students at the School of American Ballet at Lincoln Center, the official academy of the New York City Ballet. Many of these children live at the school and go home during summer and winter holidays. During the day, they attend both regular academic classes and ballet class.

At SAB, a pianist always accompanies each class to help develop the dancers' musicality and to give the instructor freedom to be spontaneous and literally compose each element of the class as it is happening. Class time is often longer than in beginning levels. Advanced students commit themselves to taking classes at least six days a week, often with two or three classes per day. Wow, what a workout!

Let's go visit one of these classes! We'll see the girls in advanced classes dancing in **pointe shoes** and dancing with the boys in a partnering class called **pas de deux**. These steps should not be tried without the proper training, but with enough training you'll be able to do them. Remember, never put on pointe shoes unless your teacher tells you that you are ready. You don't want to injure yourself!

Ballet classes at SAB always have a pianist.

Arabesque en l'air

arabesque

this classic, basic pose is one of my favorites. It gets its name from the ancient Greek and Moorish word "arabesque," which refers to an ornate art form with a wonderful, intricate geometric design. The **arabesque** creates a graceful, flowing line with the body. There are many variations of the arabesque, but all arabesques involve standing on one leg that is either straight or in demi-plié, with the other leg extended straight back and the arms posed gracefully.

arabesque en l'air (air-ah-besk on lair)

In **arabesque en l'air**, the back leg is lifted high behind the dancer and held perfectly straight so that it is parallel to the floor.

arabesque penchée (air-ah-besk pawn-shay)

This position is the same movement as the arabesque en l'air, but for **arabesque penchée**, the dancer doesn't stop when her leg is parallel with the floor. Instead, she continues lifting her back leg as high as she can so that it is as close to a split as possible. While she does this, she tilts her upper body slightly forward to help keep her balance. Ouch! You really have to be flexible to do arabesque penchée all the way!

I love to do this pose. It looks so graceful!

glissade

there are many different variations of **glissade** (glee-sahd). Glissade is a gliding, traveling step, or a step that moves the dancer across the floor. Some are done forward and some backward. This step is used to link other ballet steps together.

2.

1.

It is usually used before jumps or leaps. The name for this step comes from the French word "glisser," which means "to glide." The dancer starts in fifth position with her right foot in front. She demi-pliés and then slides her left foot out across the floor into second position. Then she jumps slightly off of her right foot and lands on her left foot, moving her right foot into fifth position

3.

4.

Sauté and grand jeté en avant

sauté (so-TAY)

"**Sauté**" means "to jump" in French. There are many different types of jumps in ballet. This one starts with two feet on the ground. The dancer springs up high into the air. Her legs straighten in midair before she returns to the ground.

Sauté

grand jeté en avant (grahn je-TAY on a-VAHN)

A **grand jeté en avant** is a large, horizontal jump. It is an allegro step, which means "lively." In this jump, the dancer splits her legs while jumping in the air, and then lands on one foot. Her arms may be in different positions, but she always looks relaxed as she moves upward. Look at her! She makes it look so easy, as though she is suspended in air! Wow, what a huge leap!

Grand jeté

grand battement and battement frappé

grand battement
(grahn baht-MAHN)

"**Grand battement**" is French for "big kick." The dancer kicks her leg up as high as she can while keeping it straight. This exercise strengthens the back and stomach. The dancer begins in either first position or fifth position. She keeps her left arm on the barre as she slides her right foot into tendu front and raises her right leg up as high as possible in a turned-out position. Then she lowers her leg, bringing it back to fifth position.

Grand battement

battement frappé
(baht-MAHN fra-PAY)

The strike of the foot in the **battement frappé** may look simple, but it requires great detail and fine-tuning. The foot must strike quickly and sharply against the floor as the leg stretches out.

The dancer begins in fifth position, with her left hand on the barre and her right foot wrapped in front of her left ankle. She brushes her right foot down so the ball of her foot strikes the floor. Then she points her right foot hard as she briskly straightens her right knee straight, lifting her leg up into the air a few inches. She finishes by bending her right knee and setting her foot down behind her left ankle, and then wrapping it at her ankle.

Battement frappé

pirouette and Spotting

pirouette (peer-WET)

The **pirouette** is a complete turn on one foot, on pointe or demi-pointe. The dancer must make a complete 360-degree turn while balancing on one leg! The body is held strong and well centered over the supporting leg. The hips and shoulders must be well aligned. The back is strongly held. The arms provide the momentum required to spin the body. Pirouettes usually begin in fifth, fourth, or second position. This is a pirouette from fourth position.

spotting

When dancers do a turn, they use a technique called **spotting** to keep themselves from getting dizzy. The dancer looks at one point across the room for as long as she can while she is turning. When she has turned so far that she must move her head, she quickly snaps her head around and refocuses on the spotting point.

1.

attitude en dedans and attitude en bas

Attitude en dedans

In **attitude** (ah-tee-TUDE), the working leg is raised and bent from the knee at an angle of 90 degrees, then turned out so that the knee is at the same level as the foot. Attitude can be done from the front, side, or back. This is one of my favorite positions. Look, you can see me doing it now! How do you like my costume?

attitude en dedans (ah-tee-TUDE on duh-DAHN)

The dancer's leg is in attitude in the front of the body.

attitude en bas (ah-tee-TUDE on bah)

The dancer's leg is in attitude in the back of the body.

Attitude en bas

pointe Work

pointe shoes

Many little girls dream of having pretty pink satin pointe shoes. But before you can start **pointe work**, your feet have to be very strong and developed. This happens only after many years of serious training. A girl usually gets her first pair of pointe shoes at eleven or twelve years old, and only under the direct supervision of her instructor. Never buy pointe shoes to try at home. They should not be worn without professional supervision by a qualified ballet instructor.

Ballet dancers sew their own ribbons onto their shoes so that each pair is an exact fit. Professional ballerinas can go through a pair of shoes in a day, so dancers have dozens of shoes at any one time!

Allyssa puts on her pointe shoes.

Now it's time for Allyssa to put rosin on her shoes.

rosin (RAH-zen)

When dancers are preparing to go on pointe, they rub their shoes in **rosin**, which is a crumbly powder that turns white and rough when the dancer steps into it. Rosin is actually dried sap from a fir tree. It helps make a ballerina's shoes less slippery when she is doing difficult pointe work.

Sous-sus and Échappé relevé

SOUS-SUS (SUE-SUE)

Sous-sus is basically a relevé in a tight fifth position, with one foot almost on top of the other foot. The feet are touching and the ankles are crossed with the dancer on pointe or demi-pointe.

échappé relevé (ay-shapp-ay rel-ah-vay)

Translated from French, "**échappé**" means "to escape" and "**relevé**" means "raised." This movement starts from fifth position and "escapes" into second or fourth position relevé, with the heels raised off the floor. This move can be done in demi-pointe or on pointe. In this case it is done on pointe. Échappé relevé is one of the most basic warm-ups for pointe work. In échappé relevé, the dancer looks as if she is gliding quickly and lightly on the tips of her toes.

Échappé relevé

Boys Technique Class
tour en l'air and Sauté passé

Tour en l'air

At SAB, boys and girls take separate classes starting at around nine years old. Although both boys and girls learn all of the basic ballet positions and steps, the boys must work on developing strong legs for big jumps and upper body strength to lift the girls in pas de deux steps. That means that what they do in class is somewhat different from what girls do. Let's take a quick trip to a boys class to see them working on jumps.

tour en l'air (tour on lair)

Tour en l'air, which involves a complete 360-degree turn or multiple turns in midair, is usually performed by men. The dancer starts in fifth position with the right foot front. He demi-pliés, rises straight up into the air, makes a turn, and then lands in fifth with the left foot front. The arms help to power the turn. The head spots as in a pirouette to prevent the dancer from getting dizzy.

sauté passé (so-TAY pah-SAY)

Sauté passé is a passé while jumping. The dancer jumps up on one leg. The foot of the other leg passes up the front of the straight leg until it reaches the knee and then slides down the back of the leg. The dancer lands on two feet.

Sauté passé

Putting it all Together

choreography basics and advanced class work

1.

When steps are linked together, they form a dance. That's called **choreography**. Choreography is very important to ballet. Each ballet starts with two people, the **composer** and the **choreographer**. The composer is hired first to write the music, or the choreographer selects a piece of music that has already been composed. Then it's the choreographer's turn. A performance on stage is basically many ballet steps linked together. The order the steps are put together in helps the dancers to express the music through their movements and to tell a story.

There are different dances for different kinds of music and occasions. The **waltz**, **mazurka**, **march**, and **pas de deux** are several standard types of dances choreographers use to create ballets.

Waltzes can be slow or fast paced and can be used for happy or sad dances. Mazurkas are fast moving, and are meant for celebrations or happy occasions. Marches are quick dances used for big ceremonies.

A pas de deux is a dance for two, usually a man and a woman. Your teacher will teach you how to put a series of steps together to create a dance. Combining several movements together is called **enchaînement** (on-shayn-mon), which means "linking together."

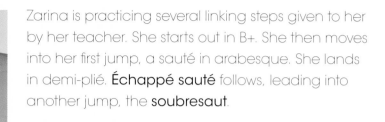

Zarina is practicing several linking steps given to her by her teacher. She starts out in B+. She then moves into her first jump, a sauté in arabesque. She lands in demi-plié. **Échappé sauté** follows, leading into another jump, the **soubresaut**.

"Soubresaut" is French for "sudden leap." The dancer both jumps from and lands in fifth position, with her legs tightly crossed and her feet pointed in the air.

2.

3.

4.

5.

pas de deux

dancers who are taking intermediate or advanced technique classes in most major ballet schools learn pair work called **pas de deux** (pah duh duh). The boys must be strong and able to lift the girls gracefully and seemingly effortlessly. The girls, on the other hand, need to be strong in their legs, feet, and arms for the difficult lifts and balances they do.

Pas de deux supported arabesque

In pas de deux, the boy and girl practice dancing together. They learn to dance in harmony with each other, coordinating their movements with their partner and feeling each other's rhythm.

pas de deux

Zarina and Lars are in pas de deux class.
They are practicing dancing together.

Lars supports Zarina in
arabesque penchée.

Lars lunges in fourth position
and supports Zarina in
arabesque penchée.

Lars stands in fourth position while holding Zarina in attitude croisé.

In the dressing room

Zarina is putting on her eyeliner.

Come meet Zarina. She is getting ready for her performance of **Coppélia**. This ballet is the story of a man who falls in love with a beautiful doll named *Coppélia*, who he tries to magically bring to life so that they may be married and live happily ever after. Through makeup and costume, Zarina is going to make herself look just like a character in the ballet.

Zarina is applying the finishing touches to her makeup.

First Zarina has to go to the dressing room and put her hair back in a tight bun. Then she has to put on special makeup called **stage makeup**. Dancers always do their hair and makeup before they put on their costumes so they do not accidentally get the costumes dirty. Stage makeup is much thicker and brighter than makeup a grown-up would wear in real life. This is because the strong stage lights make faces look pale and hard to see. Using heavy makeup helps the audience to see facial expressions from far away and figure out what dancers are thinking and feeling.

Getting into Costume

Coppélia is one of my favorite ballets.

The wardrobe mistress is helping Zarina put on her costume to make sure it fits just right.

Costumes are a big part of any ballet. A costume is worn for many performances each year, so they are sewn to be strong, comfortable for dancing, and durable. Dance companies often perform the same ballets year after year, so they need their costumes to last through many years worth of dancing. Many ballet companies have costume shops that design and make costumes for their dancers. The costume is my favorite part of any performance, especially when it's a tutu!

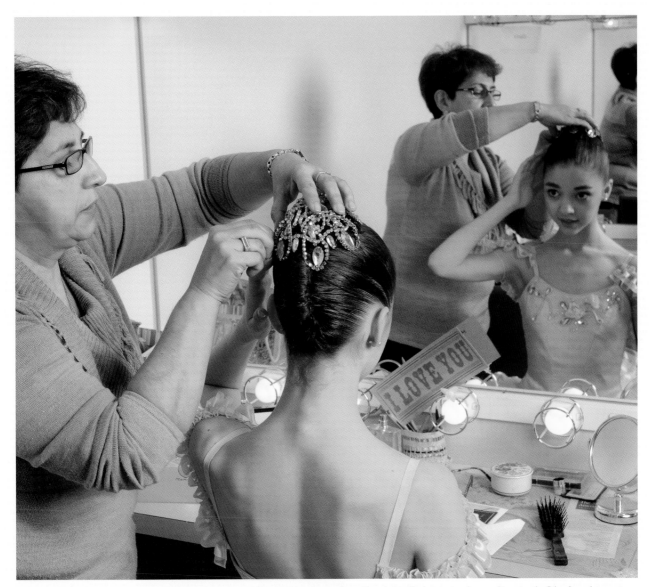

Now it's time for the headpiece to be adjusted. She's almost ready for her performance. Look at how perfect she looks!

The **wardrobe mistress** adjusts the costumes to fit each dancer perfectly, and cares for them in every way. In fact, this costume belongs to the New York City Ballet, and the wardrobe mistress has to go wherever it goes, sort of like a costume bodyguard. These costumes are one of a kind, handmade, and need her constant attention.

Warming Up

Zarina is doing warm-ups and practicing a few steps in the studio before the performance begins. Dancers always warm up before performing so they do not hurt themselves. Once she's done, the music will start and it's time to go on stage for *Coppélia*!

Dancers wish one another good luck right before a performance.

Good luck, Zarina!

fini

Wasn't that beautiful? Thanks for joining me on this magical ballet journey! My friends in Creative Movement and SAB and I really enjoyed showing you how to do ballet.

Now go put on your own tutu or leotard and whirl and twirl to some fabulous music in your own home. Better yet, sign up for a real ballet class in your hometown today!

Remember, until next time . . . keep on dreaming and keep on dancing!

Bye for now!

Glossary

Arabesque: A movement that involves standing on one leg that is either straight or in demi-plié with the other leg extended back and the arms posed gracefully.

Arabesque en l'air: A variation of the arabesque in which the back leg is lifted so that it is parallel to the floor.

Arabesque penchée: A variation of the arabesque in which the back leg is lifted as high as possible while the upper body is tilted slightly forward to help the dancer maintain her balance.

Attitude: A position in which the working leg is raised, bent from the knee at an angle of 90 degrees, and turned out so that the knee is at the same level as the foot. This position can be done from the front, side, or back.

Attitude en bas: An attitude in which the leg is in the back of the body.

Attitude en dedans: An attitude in which the leg is in the front of the body.

B+ pose: A position in which the dancer stands on either foot with the other leg behind her. Her rear leg is slightly bent and placed behind the standing foot with her knees touching. The big toe on the back foot touches the floor.

Barre: A long, rounded piece of wood attached to the walls of a ballet studio (or on freestanding supports) that dancers hold on to for support during "barre exercises."

Battement: A beating action of the extended or bent leg.

Battement frappé: A movement in which the dancer begins in fifth position with her left hand on the barre and her right foot wrapped in front of her left anklebone. She brushes her right foot down so the ball of her foot strikes the floor. Next she points her right foot hard and briskly straightens her right knee, lifting her leg up into the air a few inches. She finishes by bending her right knee and setting her foot down behind her left ankle and then wrapping it at the ankle.

Battement tendu: An exercise done at the barre in which the leg is extended to the front, side, or back. When the leg is fully extended, the knee should be straight with the foot pointed.

Center work: Exercises performed in the center of the room without support from the barre.

Choreographer: An artist who creates dances by arranging steps to music.

Choreography: The way in which dance steps are combined to create a visual expression of the music.

Circle time: The beginning of a Creative Movement class. This is when the teacher greets the students and lets them know what they will be doing in class.

Composer: A person who writes music.

Coppélia: A comic ballet about a man who falls in love with a beautiful doll named Coppélia.

Corps de ballet: Dancers in a ballet company who perform the group dances as opposed to solo parts.

Costume: An outfit that is worn on stage.

Creative movement class: A class for young dancers that encourages free and creative movement to music.

Croisé: A position in which the dancer faces front and turns her body to the left. She tendus with her right foot while holding her arms in fourth position with her left arm over her head and her head tilted to the right.

Demi-plié: A half-bend of the knees.

Développé: A movement in which a dancer stands in fifth position and slides one foot up the front of the other leg to the knee. She then extends her leg as her arms are raised. The leg is held still for a moment and then lowered.

Écarté: A position in which the dancer's body faces one corner of the room with her leg pointed to the other corner and her arms in fourth position, with her head looking behind the raised arm.

Échappé: A French term that means "to escape." A movement in which the feet move in a level manner from a closed to an open position.

Échappé relevé: A move in which the dancer demi-pliés in fifth position then springs quickly up into second or fourth position on pointe or demi-pointe. The dancer then reverses the movement and brings the legs back into fifth position demi-plié.

Échappé sauté: A jump in which the dancer springs from fifth position and lands in demi-plié with the feet opened in second position, then springs into the air again and closes the legs back to fifth position, landing in demi-plié.

Effacé: A position in which the dancer faces front and turns her body to the left. She tendus with her left foot while holding her arms in fourth position with her right arm over her head and her head tilted to the right.

En face: Any position in which the dancer's body completely faces the front of the room.

Enchaînement: The linking together of several dance movements.

Fifth position arms: A position in which the arms are lifted over the head. The arms are rounded, with the elbows slightly bent and the hands held close together but without the fingers touching.

Fifth position legs: A position in which one foot is placed in front of the other, with both feet touching and the toes of each foot lined up with the heel of the other.

First position arms: A position in which the arms are curved in front of the body and held as if they are forming a circle.

First position legs: A position in which the balls of the feet are turned out completely so that the heels touch each other and the feet face outward, trying to form a straight line.

Fourth position arms: A position in which one arm is held forward and rounded at the same height as the chest, and the other arm is raised above the head and slightly rounded.

Fourth position legs: A position in which the feet are placed as in fifth position but separated by the length of one foot.

Glissade: A gliding step that moves the dancer across the floor and links other ballet steps together. The dancer begins in fifth position with her right foot in front. She demi-pliés and then slides her left foot out across the floor into second position. She jumps slightly off of her right foot and lands on her left foot, then moves her right foot into fifth position.

Grand battement: A step in which the dancer begins in either first position or fifth position with her left arm on the barre. She slides her right foot into tendu front and raises her right leg up as high as possible in a turned-out position. She then lowers her leg, bringing it back to first or fifth position.

Grand jeté en avant: A large, horizontal jump in which the dancer splits her legs while jumping in the air and then lands on one foot.

Grand plié: A full bend of the knees. The heels are lifted when the full bend is reached (except in the second position, where they remain on the floor) and are then pushed back down to the floor as the dancer passes through a demi-plié and straightens the knees.

March: A formal, celebratory type of music or dance in which steps and beats are kept at a steady pace.

Mazurka: A fast-moving dance used in celebratory or happy scenes.

Musicality: A sensitivity to music.

Pantomime: A set of gestures used in ballet to tell a story, explain events, or show specific ideas or feelings.

Pas de chat: A movement starting in fifth position in which the dancer looks in the direction she is moving, lifts her back foot to her calf and pliés on the front leg. Then she jumps into the air, picking up both legs at once underneath her body and pointing her feet toward each other. She lands on one bent leg with her other leg pointing to the mid-shin and finishes in fifth position.

Pas de deux: A dance performed by two people.

Passé: Both a position and a movement. As a position, one leg is turned out and bent at the knee with the foot placed in front or in back of the other knee. As a movement, the working foot—the foot that is moving—slides up the front of the standing leg until the toe reaches the knee, and then the foot passes to the back of the knee and slides back down to fifth position.

Pirouette: A turn on one leg done on pointe or on demi-pointe.

Plié: An exercise in which the dancer bends her knees and then straightens them.

Pointe shoe: A type of ballet shoe used by advanced dancers that has special reinforcements in the toe and sole so that a ballerina can stand on her toes while dancing.

Pointe work: Dancing that occurs on the tips of the toes. This is performed in pointe shoes.

Positions: There are five basic foot positions in ballet. There are also five basic arm positions.

Relevé: A movement in which the dancer rises to demi-pointe or pointe. The dancer begins in first or fifth position and smoothly lifts both of her heels as far off the floor as she can. When she reaches the balls of her feet, or arrives on pointe, she slowly goes back down and ends again in first or fifth position.

Révérence: A bow or curtsy.

Rond de jambe à terre: A movement in which the leg is rotated in a circular pattern. The dancer begins in first position with her left hand on the barre and glides her right foot to tendu front, side, and then back.

Rond de jambe en dedans: A version of the rond de jambe in which the foot does the reverse movements, starting with tendu back.

Rosin: A susbstance made from the sap of a pine tree that dancers rub on their shoes to make them less slippery and safer for difficult pointe work.

Sauté: A step in which the dancer begins with two feet on the ground, then pliés and springs high into the air. Her legs straighten in midair before she returns to the ground in demi-plié.

Sauté passé: A move in which the dancer jumps up on one leg. The foot of the other leg passes up the front of the straight leg until it reaches the knee and then slides down the back of the leg and lands on two feet.

School of American Ballet (SAB): The official academy of the New York City Ballet, founded in 1934 by the famous choreographer George Balanchine and supporter of the arts Lincoln Kirstein. SAB is located in New York City at Lincoln Center.

Second position arms: A position in which the arms are opened to the dancer's sides with the elbows slightly rounded as in first position.

Second position legs: A position in which the balls of both feet are turned out completely, with the heels separated by the length of one foot.

Soubresaut: A jump in which the dancer both takes off from and lands in fifth position with the legs tightly crossed and feet pointed in the air.

Sous-sus: A position in which the dancer relevés in a tight fifth position, with one foot almost on top of the other foot. The feet are touching and the ankles are crossed with the dancer on pointe or demi-pointe.

Spotting: A technique used by dancers to keep themselves from getting dizzy when turning.

Stage makeup: Heavy makeup used by performers which serves to accentuate the features of a performer on a brightly lit stage.

Sur le cou-de-pied: A position in which the working foot is wrapped around the ankle of the other leg.

Tempo: The speed or pace of a piece of music.

Third position arms: A position in which one arm is curved over the head, as in fifth position, and the other is held to the side, as in second position.

Third position legs: A position in which one foot is placed in front of the other foot. The heel of the front foot should touch the middle of the back foot.

Tour en l'air: A jump that involves a complete 360-degree turn or multiple turns in midair. The dancer starts in fifth position. He demi-pliés and pushes off the floor into the air and makes a complete turn (or two) before landing on the floor in fifth position demi-plié.

Turnout: The turning out of the legs and feet from the hips. With perfect turnout, in first position a dancer's toes point in opposite directions from each other to form a straight line, with the heels touching.

Waltz: Music or dance performed in counts of three with a strong accent on the first beat.

Wardrobe mistress: The person who alters costumes to fit each dancer, and cares for the costumes in every way.

Working foot: The foot that is moving during a dance step.

Index